The Main Idea Strategy:
Improving Reading Comprehension Through Inferential Thinking

Student Practice Materials

Second Edition

Daniel J. Boudah, Ph.D.

with Pamela A. Boudah, M.S.Ed.

The Main Idea Strategy: Improving Reading Comprehension Through Inferential Thinking
(Student Practice Materials) 2nd edition
© Daniel J. Boudah, 2012, 2008

ISBN: 978-0-578-07233-3

Distributed by Lulu.com

Acknowledgments

This work would not have been possible or be complete without several acknowledgments. Thanks be to God. You make all things possible. In truth, you are able to do exceedingly, abundantly far more than I could ask for or think of (Eph. 3:20). Many thanks to Daniel Barnes, teacher and graduate student. Thanks for taking some of my ideas and crafting drafts of some of the material. Thanks also to our son, Jeremy, for your ideas that led to some of the topical passages. Thank you, Drs. Don Deshler and Jean Schumaker: You are my mentors and my heroes.

About the Authors

Daniel J. Boudah is an associate professor at East Carolina University. Dr. Boudah previously taught general and special education in public schools. He has been awarded federal and other grants, and has carried out school-based research in numerous areas. He has published work in professional journals, textbooks, and newsletters, and he has developed teacher- training materials. His work has been nationally recognized for excellence by the Council for Exceptional Children, the Council for Learning Disabilities, and the American Educational Research Association. He is a past president of the Council for Learning Disabilities. Dr. Boudah's continuing professional interests include programs and services for low-performing students and students with disabilities, learning and instructional strategies, dropout prevention, teacher collaboration, and systems change.

Pamela A. Boudah is an educator and marketing consultant. She has a B.S. in business administration and a M.S.Ed. in educational psychology and research. Pamela has worked in marketing and directed computer technology programs at the high school and college levels. She has presented at national and international conferences, including the American Educational Research Association.

Table of Contents

How to Use the Materials in This Book

The Main Idea Strategy consists of five steps: (1) Make the Topic known, (2) Accent at least two Essential Details, (3) Ink out the Clarifying Details, (4) Notice how the Essential Details are related, and (5) Infer the Main Idea. The steps are easily remembered with the first-letter mnemonic device "MAIN-I."

Effectively teaching the strategy to students, however, entails far more than just introducing them to the steps of the strategy. Based on a research project focused on the Main Idea Strategy, as well as the work of Schumaker and Deshler and colleagues on learning strategy instruction, the *Teacher Instructional Manual* for the Main Idea Strategy includes five sections: Getting Started, Instructional Lessons, Student Practice Lessons, Closure, and Scoring. The third section of that manual, Student Practice Lessons, has two parts: Guidelines for Controlled Practice and Guidelines for Grade-Level Practice. The Guidelines for Controlled Practice provide you with detailed directions for effectively using the practice materials included in this *Student Practice Materials* book.

The *Student Practice Materials* book contains 24 practice passages and comprehension questions associated with each passage. (Answer Keys appear in the *Teacher Instructional Manual*.) In this book, all of the student practice passages are arranged in order of Flesch-Kincaid readability levels, from the lowest to the highest. The passages begin at about the second-grade level and progress to the ninth-grade level. The number of words per passage and the readability level are printed in the bottom right-hand corner of each passage page (e.g., 325/4.6). The intention is that you can guide students through using increasingly more difficult materials before prompting them to use the strategy with regular classroom materials or other materials. There are three practice passages at each grade level so that if a student does not reach mastery (i.e., earn a score of 80% or above) on one of the three passages, you have additional practice materials available.

Like the pretest, there are two parts to each controlled practice attempt. In Part 1, students read and highlight Essential Details within paragraphs in a passage. They also paraphrase the inferred main idea of each paragraph. In the second part, students recall information from the passage and complete comprehension questions. **The two parts may be completed on the same day, or the comprehension questions may be completed the day immediately following the highlighting and Main Idea paraphrasing activity.**

Follow the lesson guidelines for each controlled practice attempt. The suggested mastery level is 80% for each assessment measure. That means that before you allow a student to progress to passages with a higher readability level, the student should earn a score of 80% or above when highlighting Essential Details, 80% or above when paraphrasing Main Ideas, and 80% or above when answering the comprehension questions. (You can certainly set a higher standard if you wish.) In other words, if you start a student with the passage entitled "A New Man," written at the 3.0 (third-grade) readability level, make sure the student earns scores of 80% or above on a passage at the third-grade level before you allow the student to practice using the strategy on a passage at the 4.0 level. As noted, there are several practice passages at each grade level that can be used for practicing to mastery.

That said, please keep in mind three things. One, **this is not an instructional program for teaching students decoding or word-attack skills**, and therefore a) you will have to use other materials to teach decoding skills, and b) weaker performance in decoding may limit the number of passages that you can use at progressively higher readability levels.

Second, remember that, **if students are not reaching mastery using the included passages at any grade level, you can seek out additional commercially available passages written at that level.** For example, if a student is not reaching mastery while reading the passages written at the fifth-grade level, then you should (a) carefully analyze the errors made by the student, (b) reteach and demonstrate the strategy for clearer student understanding, and (c) seek out additional practice passages at the fifth-grade level. This instructional sequence would be far more effective than simply allowing the student to work with passages written at the sixth- or seventh-grade level. For additional short passages, the *Timed Readings* Series is recommended. You can find information about this series at <http://www.glencoe.com/gln/jamestown/reading_rate/timed_readings.php>.

Third, please keep in mind that you should **initiate controlled practice activities with each student with passages that are written at a readability level that is slightly below the student's current reading performance level.** That is, if a student is currently reading at the fifth-grade level, select passages at the third- or fourth-grade level for initial controlled practice activities. Working with easy passages will build student confidence, while at the same time allowing each student the opportunity to become proficient at using the strategy with initially less challenging reading.

Instructions for scoring student attempts at highlighting Essential Details and paraphrasing Main Ideas are found in the *Main Idea Strategy Teacher Instructional Manual*, as well as a scoring example, and answer keys for all student practice materials.

I trust that you will find success using the materials in this book. If you have suggestions, find obvious errors, or have success stories that you would like to share with me, I would appreciate hearing from you. You can email me at boudahd@ecu.edu or dboudah@nc.rr.com.

Best wishes,

Daniel J. Boudah, Ph.D.
East Carolina University

Student Practice Materials

Name _____   Date _____

Passage #1: Mr. Plain

John Plain woke up every morning at six. He'd wake up, get his wife up, and check on the dog. Every day, they would eat plain cereal with skim milk. Monday through Friday, Mr. Plain wore clean white shirts without a speck. He'd wear the same type of pants every day, too. Mr. Plain brushed his teeth for exactly two minutes. On the way to work, he would pick up some coffee. Mr. Plain had a good life.

One day, John Plain started to think. He thought of what he could do. He thought about what he should not do. He thought about getting a tattoo. His wife said, "It's not for you." Should he quit his job? No, he could not be a slob. Long hair in the back? Not unless he wanted to live alone in a shack. What could he do?

Then an idea came to his mind. This was an idea that nobody would mind! He decided not to shave. That was like his friend Dave. But John wanted more. Simple hair would be a bore! He didn't shave the next night. He didn't shave for many a night! The hair grew, and it grew. It covered his lip, and it would not quit.

Weeks went by. Mr. Plain did not trim the hair above his lip. It curled down his chest. Some people thought he was lazy. Some thought he was a little crazy! His wife started to frown. "Good grief," his wife said. "Please cut that mustache. It will be a relief." She said that very, very loud.

A year went by. Mr. Plain had more friends at work. It wasn't all about the mustache. He was just pretty funny! The mustache was four feet long. Mr. Plain said it was long enough! He decided to get it cut. His life was less boring. He had learned a lot. He could be interesting on his own. He did not need a device.

332/2.5

Name _____   Date   _____

Passage #1 Comprehension Questions

Mr. Plain

1) In the first paragraph, how interesting does Mr. Plain's life seem?

2) What did Mr. Plain's wife say would happen if Mr. Plain grew long hair in the back?

3) What does Mr. Plain choose to do to change his life?

4) About how long did Mr. Plain go without cutting his mustache?

5) By the end of the story, what does Mr. Plain learn about his ability to be interesting?

Name _____   Date   _____

Passage #2: Look at the Cars!

Look at the cars! Look at the trucks! Look at the buses! They are on every road. Some are big and long. Some are short and fat. Some are in between. A few are very long.

Some cars are small. Only two people can ride inside them. They are also light. That helps. They do not need much gas to go. Drivers do not spend much on gas. That's a good thing.

Do you like sports cars? They can be bigger than other cars. A Mustang is a sports car. Sports cars have big engines. The engines are strong. They can go over 100 miles per hour. That's fast!

School buses are very long. Some are up to 50 feet long. Fifty kids can ride on a bus. A bus takes kids to places. Sometimes they go to school. Sometimes they go on trips. Then many cars are not needed.

Many trucks are on the road. Most are bigger than cars. They are not as big as buses. Sometimes only two or three people can fit in them. Trucks have beds in the back. They can carry things to places. People do not ride in truck beds. A big truck can carry lots of things. Many things are put in stores.

211/2.9

Name _____   Date   _____

Passage #2 Comprehension Questions

Look at the Cars!

1) What is one good thing about driving a small car?

2) How fast can a sports car go?

3) What is the name of one sports car mentioned?

4) How many kids could ride on a school bus?

5) What is the purpose of most trucks?

Name _____   Date _____

Passage #3: The Frozen Monster

I looked out my bedroom window. "Snow!" I yelled. A huge blanket of snow had fallen on the earth. It was awesome. The trees were covered. Dad's car looked as if it was a mound of cotton candy. I couldn't even see the front steps or the mailbox. I got on my coat and boots and ran out the front door.

"Crunch! Crunch!" I heard noises as my boots hit the soft snow. I walked along and heard another sound. It must have been ice falling. I walked on. Just then, I felt the ground shake. Then a pile of snow started to move. I started to sweat. The snow moved again. My sweat froze.

Suddenly, a giant snow monster jumped out of the snow. The monster yelled. I froze in my tracks. The snow monster grabbed me. I was able to get out of his hands. I ran into Ted, my older brother. He started to run, too. The snow monster followed. The monster grew bigger. He was picking up snow from the ground. The monster grew, and grew, and grew!

We ran into our house. The snow monster ran up to the door. He stopped and stood there. He was angry and hollering. We hid in our warm, cozy house. The snow monster banged on the door. The door came open. The cold air made us shiver, but the snow monster started to drip. He also started to get smaller.

The snow monster got angry. He picked up my mom's car and threw it. Then the sun started to come out. It started to get warmer outside. Thirty degrees. Forty degrees. The snow monster tried to put more snow onto his body. Drip, drip, drip! Then, the snow monster turned to mush. He couldn't move. He then turned into harmless water.

303/2.9

Name _____   Date   _____

Passage #3: Comprehension Questions

The Frozen Monster

1) At the beginning of the story, what was the weather like?

2) How did the snow monster get larger?

3) Where did the main character and his brother hide from the snow monster?

4) Why did the snow monster first start to melt?

5) What led to the end of the snow monster?

Name _____   Date _____

Passage #4: Angelfish

Angelfish live in the waters of South America. They live in warm seas and coral reefs. They can grow to be 17 inches long. They usually swim alone or in pairs. They have thin bodies. They also have a strong spine in the lower part of the cheekbone. The angelfish are one of the most brightly colored fish of the sea. They mainly eat sponge and algae.

There is a fish called the blackspot angelfish. It can change from girl to boy. No, it cannot do it by wishing to become a boy. It happens for a reason.

The fish live in groups. Each group has one boy fish and four girl fish. The boy is blue. The four girl fish are yellow.

The boy angelfish is the strongest and largest member of the group. He is the one who protects and looks after the girls. When the boy dies, the group needs a new fish in charge. This is when the largest girl fish in the group begins to change the way she looks.

The girl begins to grow larger. After a week, she starts changing from yellow to blue. Slowly, she begins to act like a boy. After two weeks, black stripes come on her body. This shows that the change is complete. She is now a boy!

220/3.4

Name _____   Date _____

Passage #4 Comprehension Questions

Angelfish

1) What color is the boy angelfish?

2) Which kind of angelfish is the strongest?

3) Why does an angelfish change from a girl to a boy?

4) What happens to the largest girl when she changes?

5) Where do angelfish live?

Name _____   Date   _____

Passage #5: Mrs. Freeman

Mrs. Freeman was a teacher. Students said she was nice. Many parents had her as a teacher. They said she was nice, too. Many teachers came to her for ideas. The principal said she should win an award.

One day, Tonya called Mrs. Freeman old. Tonya blushed. Mrs. Freeman told her it was okay. The teacher then heard students talking about her age. She asked, "How old do you think I am?" She did not get mad when one student said, "A hundred!"

Later, Mrs. Freeman was out of school. The principal came in the class. He asked the students what they liked about Mrs. Freeman. Jose said he liked when they got to use drawings in class. David said he liked when they used blocks in math. Brittany said she liked when they sang and danced.

During the last week of school, Mrs. Freeman said she was retiring. Some children cried. Some put their heads down. Others wanted to run away from the class. No one said anything.

On the last day, there was a knock on the door. Mrs. Freeman saw the hallway filled with adults. They all had had Mrs. Freeman as a teacher. Each had food and presents in their hands. There was lots of laughing and crying. Mrs. Freeman told funny stories. Everyone wished her well.

221/3.9

Name _____   Date _____

Passage #5 Comprehension Questions

Mrs. Freeman

1) What is Mrs. Freeman's job?

2) How do most people feel about Mrs. Freeman?

3) What are two reasons why students have fun in Mrs. Freeman's classroom?

4) How do students react when Mrs. Freeman says she is retiring?

5) What is the surprise party really about?

Name _____   Date   _____

Passage #6: Your Phone is Ringing

Cell phones are everywhere today. It didn't used to be that way. Only less than twenty years ago, few people owned one. It seems like longer than that. They were expensive to use. They cost hundreds of dollars each month. They didn't work in a lot of places. They were big and clunky, too.

Flip phones are still very popular. They seem to be all over the place. Have you seen some of the latest kinds of cell phones? You can get slide phones. Those can be kind of cool. You can own a phone that has a full keyboard. It's very small though.

Business people use cell phones to stay connected with work. You can take pictures or video. Lots of people use their phones to download music. Some are even getting rid of their own portable music devices. Making calls is nice, but email can be good to have on a cell phone, too. Many people send emails and surf the Internet as well. You can even have your calendar on your phone.

Red, yellow, green. Stripes, pictures, clear. I have seen lots of different- looking cell phones. Cell phones used to come just in grey or black. How boring! You can even change the color of your phone. You just buy a different plate for it.

Yes, cell phones are everywhere. People use them to call home or friends. People can use them if they have an emergency. What I don't like is when I hear ringing during a movie! How about if you are at a restaurant? Don't you hate it when someone next to you is talking really loud on their phone? Some doctors tell people not to use cell phones in their offices. It can also be scary when people drive while talking on the phone. That's not good.

305/3.9

Name _____   Date _____

Passage #6 Comprehension Questions

Your Phone Is Ringing

1) What are two reasons why many people didn't used to have cell phones?

2) What is one bad thing about having a keyboard on a cell phone?

3) What are at least two popular features on cell phones?

4) In the past, most cell phones came in only two colors. What were they?

5) Where are at least two places where people should not use cell phones?

Name _____   Date   _____

Passage #7: Becoming a Pilot

There you are, soaring through the clouds. The ground is thousands of feet below. You're not a bird. You're not a plane. You are an airplane pilot. You've studied hard. You've paid the money. You've passed the tests. You've kept yourself healthy. You have prepared yourself for this day. Now you can actually fly.

How do you get a pilot's license? First, you have to apply for flight school. There are various schools. Some people learn to fly after joining the military. You have to study some information in books. You have to attend some classes. You have to pass some hard tests. You also have to fly a certain number of hours with an instructor. It's a lot like getting a license to drive a car.

It's good to know a little math as a pilot. You can use math to figure out the costs of the initial training. For example, you may need to figure out the cost of 60 hours of training, as well as the gas and oil. It is important to be able to determine the speed of the aircraft. If you can do that, you can know when to slow down before landing. Another important use of math is in calculating wind speed. That way, you can know whether there might be turbulence. Then a pilot can tell passengers to be prepared.

You may think that airplane computers do all the math. What if the on-board computer system goes down? Do you start to sweat? Do you panic? No, a pilot can still calculate velocity and wind speed. He or she can then still fly and land the plane safely. Wouldn't that be a little less stressful?

What if you were flying on a plane with a really sick pilot? What if her eyesight was going bad? There is another thing that some may not know about being a pilot. You have to pass regular health exams. As a pilot, staying in shape is important for you as well as others.

337/4.5

Name _____   Date   _____

Passage #7 Comprehension Questions

Becoming a Pilot

1) What is the first thing you need to do to become a pilot?

2) Besides attending some classes and passing some tests, what is another important part of gaining your pilot's license?

3) What are two things that a pilot can do with a little knowledge of math?

4) What is another good reason for pilots to know some math?

5) Besides the pilot, who else depends on the pilot's good health?

Name _____   Date _____

Passage #8: Going to the Moon

Do you think that people will ever fly to Mars? That may seem crazy. At one time, many people thought that a man on the moon was like that. They said it couldn't be done. It was only in the movies. Getting to the moon didn't turn out to be so crazy after all.

In the 1950s, scientists built rockets that might fly to the moon. At the time, many people wondered about it. Could we really get to the moon? Why do we want to get there? How will we safely fly to the moon? These were hard questions.

At that time, many people wanted new ideas. John F. Kennedy then became president. He was young and hopeful about the future. When Kennedy spoke, people listened. Many believed him. He told people that the United States would get to the moon.

Many people then thought we could get to the moon. Scientists worked hard, but Kennedy never got to see people get to the moon. He was killed by someone. It was a sad day. Still, people kept working hard. NASA soon named the Florida space center after him.

In 1969, NASA sent people to the moon. The rocket was called Apollo 11. The world watched on television when the rocket landed. Neil Armstrong then stepped on the moon. He said, "That's one small step for man, one giant leap for mankind." People were very excited about it. People wondered what was next for the future.

247/4.9

Name _____   Date _____

Passage #8 Comprehension Questions

Going to the Moon

1) At first, how did most people feel about the chances of getting to the moon?

2) When did scientists begin to build rockets to try to get to the moon?

3) Why did many people like John F. Kennedy?

4) After President Kennedy died, what was named after him?

5) Who was Neil Armstrong?

Name _____   Date _____

Passage #9: Fast Food

You've just had a long day at work. You woke up at six o'clock and worked until five o'clock. Your stomach is growling, and you're tired. You're thirty minutes from your house, and you have to pick up the kids from daycare. You have no idea what's in the refrigerator. On the highway, there's a one fast food place after another. What should you do?

Collectively, restaurants that offer little more than burgers and fries and a drive-through lane are called "fast food restaurants." When you get in the drive-through lane, you can order your meal. By the time you drive around the building, the food is ready. It takes all of five minutes! Then you can drive home and eat in no time at all. It couldn't be much faster.

Most meals come as "combos," which means "combinations." You get your meat, a side order, a drink, and sometimes even a dessert. For about five dollars, a person can get a hamburger, french fries, and a soda. All you have to do is order a combo. Then your entire meal is instantly ready. You don't have to get any food or drink on your own.

Some restaurants offer toys to go along with their kids meals. For about three dollars, a kid can get a hamburger, french fries, a soda, and a plastic toy. The toys may not even be anything special to an adult, but they may be quite precious to little kids. It is easy for kids to associate toys and fun with most fast food restaurants. No wonder so many children often ask their parents to take them to fast food restaurants!

Fast food sounds like a good deal, right? Well, in 2004, someone made a movie about a guy who ate at a fast food restaurant every day for an entire month! He gained a lot of weight. That probably happened because most fast food is fried in grease, so it is usually very fattening. He also reported feeling angry, depressed, and tired. You might want to keep these things in mind if you eat fast food often.

353/4.9

Name _____   Date _____

Passage #9: Comprehension Questions

Fast Food

1) What is one reason people choose to eat at a fast food restaurant rather than cooking?

2) If you order a "combo" at a fast food place, what often comes in the order?

3) About how long does it usually take to order and receive a fast food meal?

4) Why do many children enjoy going to fast food restaurants?

5) What is one bad side effect of eating fast food?

Name _____   Date _____

Passage #10: How to Treat Pets

Have you ever tried to pick up your pet cat or dog, only to have it bite or scratch you when you touched it? If so, you might have thought at the time that your pet was angry or even mean. Perhaps there are other reasons why the pet bit you. Even if you have a very nice pet, you might have bothered it. Maybe your pet felt scared by something you did.

Think about the way you've treated your pet in the past. If you rub your dog's head, feed it, and play with it, your dog would probably like to play with you. Also, think of your pet like a person. When someone upsets you or makes you mad, don't you remember it? Pets remember things, too. If people hit their dogs a lot and are mean to them, then the dogs probably are going to avoid the person who is causing the stress.

Also, consider what would happen if you allow your pet to run in the road or bite you. The pet will likely continue to do those activities, unless you make it stop. Generally, you would have a hard time training a pet if it has spent most of its life with little or no rules. It's like the saying goes, "You can't teach an old dog new tricks."

Finally, pretend that someone reached for your dinner while you were eating. That might startle you. Now, if a dog is in the middle of eating, and you put your hand in the way, your hand might get bitten. Does that mean the dog was mean, or that you shouldn't do that? Pets cannot talk, so they react in other ways, which could include a bite or a scratch.

Have you ever heard of the Golden Rule? It is, "Treat others as you would like to be treated." If you get a pet, and it bites you or does not play with you, try to think about the Golden Rule. Think about other reasons for the pet's behavior before saying that the animal is mean.

349/5.3

Name _____   Date _____

Passage #10 Comprehension Questions

How to Treat Pets

1) Besides "being mean," what is another reason why pets may bite or scratch?

2) What are some things you could do that would make a pet want to play with you?

3) Is teaching an old and stubborn dog how to behave an easy task? Why or why not?

4) What could likely happen if you interrupt an animal during its feeding?

5) What rule should you think about before you get a pet and while you have the pet?

Name _____   Date   _____

Passage #11: M&Ms

M&Ms are small candies that are popular in many countries. They come in six different colors. Originally, these colors were purple, brown, green, yellow, orange, and red. The colors have changed a few times. In 1949, purple was taken out, and tan was put in. In 1976, red was taken out because of health concerns. By 1987, red M&Ms were put back in. In 1995, tan M&Ms were changed to blue after a vote. In 2002, purple was added back.

M&Ms are one of the most popular candies in the United States. In England, they were called *Smarties*. Forest Mars saw soldiers in the Spanish Civil War eating candy-coated chocolates. He learned that the candy coating kept the chocolate from melting. He thought that was a great idea.

M&Ms were first sold in America in 1941. In 1954, peanut M&Ms were first sold. In 1990, peanut butter M&Ms were sold. In 1996, a new kind of M&Ms was sold; they were called *M&M Minis*. In 1998, M&Ms created another new kind, called *M&M Crispies*.

A few years ago, Mars company started an advertisement called "Help the M&Ms Find Their Colors." In 1997, they had a game called "The Grey Imposter M&M Game." If you found a grey M&M, you would win a million dollars. Many people ended up finding uncolored M&Ms and thought they won. M&Ms has also sponsored a NASCAR race car driver.

M&Ms were also used in a 2004 space mission. Mike Melville opened a bag of M&Ms at the edge of space. He was conducting an experiment. He wanted to show that the candy was weightless. It's too bad that M&Ms can actually make you gain weight here on Earth. Otherwise, we'd eat them for breakfast, lunch, and dinner!

292/5.8

Name _____   Date _____

Passage #11 Comprehension Questions

M&Ms

1) How did Forest Mars discover the idea for M&Ms?

2) Why do M&Ms have a candy coating?

3) M&Ms come in how many colors?

4) What are two of the different kinds of M&Ms?

5) What are two ways that M&Ms have been advertised?

Name _____   Date _____

Passage #12: Got a Smoke?

You walk into the room and are met with a cloud of smoke. Your eyes begin to water, and you have a hard time breathing. You wonder why anyone smokes. Smoking causes health problems, makes people look bad, and wastes money. Still, people do it.

Smoking causes heart disease and cancer, including lung cancer. This can make breathing harder. The effects of smoking also are linked to many deaths. Do you want any of that?

I wonder why people think that smoking is cool. Smokers have a strong smell of tobacco. Most people don't like that. Also, smoking causes teeth to look yellow. People who smoke for a long time also have a hoarse voice and make lots of hacking noises.

In addition, smokers pay four dollars per pack of cigarettes. Most smokers use a pack or two each day. If a smoker uses a pack of cigarettes a day, that person would spend over one thousand dollars per year on a bad habit. Imagine how much money a smoker spends in ten, twenty, or even fifty years!

Did you know that smoking can be dangerous for others also? Pregnant women who smoke create a greater chance of problems for their babies. Nonsmokers who breathe in cigarette smoke are more likely to die of lung cancer also. Now that's something else to think about.

224/5.9

Name _____   Date   _____

Passage #12 Comprehension Questions

Got a Smoke?

1) What are three reasons why people should not smoke?

2) In the author's opinion, does smoking make people look "cool" or look worse?

3) How much do some smokers spend on cigarettes each year?

4) Do smokers live healthier lives than nonsmokers? Explain why or why not.

5) What is one way that smoking can also hurt others?

Name _____   Date _____

Passage #13: Have You Seen Frosty?

I love winter activities, especially building a snowman. In case you live somewhere where there isn't any snow, let me tell you how. First, make a snowball by picking up a handful of snow and packing it tightly together. Then, put the snowball down and roll it on the snow that has fallen on the ground. The snowball will get larger. Continue rolling until the snowball has gathered enough snow to make it as big as you want the head of the snowman to be. Make sure to take any pieces of grass or mulch out of the head, so your snowman looks better.

Next, make another snowball like the first one. Make sure this second snowball is larger than the first one. This second, larger snowball will become the torso or middle of the snowman.

Make a third snowball that is even bigger than the first two. This will be for the base of the snowman. Be sure that this third snowball is even larger than the second snowball. When you are finished making the third and largest snowball, carefully stack the second snowball on top of the third one. Then put the first snowball on top of the second.

After that, find two twigs or small tree branches for the snowman's arms. Carefully stick them a few inches into the sides of the middle of the snowman. Then find some dark rocks, buttons, or coal to make two eyes for the snowman. Arrange some more rocks, buttons, or coal on the head of the snowman in order to make the mouth. Find a carrot, and stick it into the center of the face to make the snowman's nose.

The last step is to find a scarf, hat, or jacket to use for the snowman's clothes. You probably should use old clothes because they will eventually get wet. Place the clothes in the appropriate places on the snowman. Now you have your own Frosty, Joe, or Susanna Snowman. Or Snowwoman.

331/6.0

Name _____   Date _____

Passage #13 Comprehension Questions

Have You Seen Frosty?

1) How many snowballs do you need to make a snowman?

2) What do you need to do so that the snowman looks good?

3) What is the importance of the third snowball?

4) What should you use to represent the arms of the snowman?

5) What can you use for the eyes and mouth of a snowman?

Name _____   Date   _____

Passage #14: Land a Computer Job

You can get a job in computers. You may not even need any training. However, your job could be sweeping the floor.

You must study hard to become a computer expert. You must read lots of computer manuals and study lots of books. You need to read lots of magazines, newspapers, and newsletters. If you want to move up in a company, you must also get formal training.

The experts often spend about two hours every day reading about computers. They have to learn what happened in the computer industry that day! The computer industry changes every day.

Computer experts spend many hours practicing what was read. They have to practice using many kinds of computers. They often swap ideas with other people who work with computers.

Computer experts choose their own hours. However, they work many hours. Your hours will never be just from 9 a.m. to 5 p.m. If you think so, you'll never become a computer expert.

160/6.7

Adapted from: Walter, R. (2000). *The Secret Guide to Computers*. Secretfun.com. Used by permission.

Name _____   Date _____

Passage # 14 Comprehension Questions

Land a Computer Job

1) Do you have to have a degree to work with computers?

2) What kinds of materials should you read to become a computer expert?

3) What kind of practice should you do to become a computer expert?

4) How many hours does the average computer expert spend reading about computers every day?

5) What is the work schedule like for a computer expert?

Name _____   Date _____

Passage #15: Your Teen Brain

Have you ever noticed that teachers make you work in a different way in high school than in elementary school? This is because your brain works differently in high school than in elementary school. Looking into how we learn shows that you really do think differently as a teenager than you did as an elementary student. As a teenager, the way you think and process information is changing. Researchers say you are in a new stage of development.

You no longer depend on a teacher, peer, or another adult to evaluate your work. Instead, you can now look at a project and analyze how well you did. You are able to think about the grade earned. You are also able to pick out the best parts of what you did on the project. You can see ways in which you can improve. Isn't it nice to be able to think more independently than younger students?

Creating your own report or project is also more possible for you now than in fourth grade. Why? You are now more reflective. You can look beyond information that you are given. This allows you to come up with cool ideas of your own. At this stage, you should be able to use teacher directions to develop your own ideas for projects. For example, a teacher should not have to give you a number of choices for a project about the favorite part of a book. You can now come up with your own ideas rather than relying on the teacher.

Students at this stage are better at thinking in another way also. You can look at situations and ask "if-then" type of questions about a problem. Think about when you see someone who you think is popular. You think that "*if*" you acted or dressed like that person, "*then*" you would also be popular. This thinking process is called "drawing conclusions."

In addition, rather than deciding that you also could be popular if you wore a red shirt like the "cool kid," you can now use logical reasoning to find out why that person is popular. This should be helpful. That is, with logical reasoning, you should be able to figure out that the kid is well liked because he is friendly, not because he wears a red shirt. Doesn't that make more sense?

390/6.9

Adapted from: Carin, A. A., & Sund, R. B. (1980). *Teaching Modern Science* (3rd ed.). Columbus, OH: Merrill. Used by permission.

Name _____   Date   _____

Passage #15 Comprehension Questions

Your Teen Brain

1) What is one difference, other than age, between young students and teenagers?

2) What are two ways that you think more independently as a teenager than as a younger student?

3) What is one difference between doing projects in elementary school and doing projects in middle or high school?

4) What must you do to answer "if-then" questions?

5) What is logical reasoning?

Name _____   Date _____

Passage #16: Do I Have to Do Homework?

I bet you do not like hearing this: "Today's homework is …" You might think that only really mean teachers give homework. It's not true. Believe it or not, teachers do not give homework to be mean. Homework does take up some of your free time, but it helps you to learn and to remember what you learn. So stop complaining!

In elementary school, kids only have a little bit of homework. It is assigned for certain reasons. For example, if you learned how to add during the school day, your homework might be a worksheet to compute some addition problems. Another common type of homework in elementary school is reading. In school, your teacher might have had your class read aloud. Then, at home, your parents would listen to you read.

By high school, homework gets more difficult and is a little different. Classes are more demanding, so teachers may give various types of homework. If you read a chapter of a new book during the day, your homework might be to read the next chapter, understand it, and be able to write and talk about it. In math, you may have to try to solve problems from a chapter you have not started yet. You have to learn more independently, but you still practice some things you learned in school.

College presents the next challenging level of homework. In college, most people are only in class for fifteen to twenty hours per week. That is like about two or three days of elementary or high school! Usually, though, college students have around fifteen to twenty hours of homework each week. For many college classes, you have to read books on your own. Then, your professor may lecture about information that is not in your books. For homework, you might then get a week or two to write essays about what you read for homework and discussed in class. In college, professors do not remind you every day to do your homework.

When you graduate from school, you must start work. After work, people usually come home and do a variety of things. Most of the time, they might cook, wash dishes, and do the laundry. People also have to take care of their children, if they have any. People have to pay bills and balance their checkbooks. These tasks may have nothing to do with school or work, but they must be done. These chores are a part of everyday life, but could be called the next type of homework.

422/7.0

Name _____   Date _____

Passage #16 Comprehension Questions

Do I Have to Do Homework?

1) Why do teachers give homework?

2) What is the purpose of homework in elementary school?

3) What are two reasons why students have to do homework in high school?

4) Why do students have so much homework in college?

5) What types of "homework" do people do after they are done with schooling?

Name _____   Date _____

Passage #17: Structure of Government

The people who wrote the Constitution were called Framers. They needed to create a government that was strong enough to rule while keeping a balance of power. The Americans remembered the English kings and were afraid of a leader that was too strong. The new Constitution tried to solve this problem. It set up a government with three branches, the legislative branch (Congress), the executive branch, and the judicial branch. It allowed each branch to check the power of the other two.

The first branch of government is Congress. It has two houses. They are called the Senate and the House of Representatives. Congress has the power to tax, to coin money, to borrow money, and to control trade. It can also set up courts and a postal system. Congress has the power to declare war, also.

The House of Representatives is the larger of the two houses. There are 435 members. The representatives are based on the population of individual states. Every state has at least one member. Members of the House of Representatives serve a two-year term. They are chosen from districts picked by their states. The Senate is the other part of Congress. There are 100 members. Each state has two senators. They are elected to six-year terms.

The House of Representatives has the power to remove federal officers. This includes the president. The Senate tries these officials. Their power is a good example of checks and balances. This is how one branch can keep the other branches, executive and judicial, from abusing their power.

The executive branch is a powerful branch. The powers of the president have grown. People look to the president for leadership. Presidents who have shown strong leadership have been the most successful presidents in history. It is the president's duty to carry out the laws and act as commander-in-chief of the Armed Forces. The president may recommend laws to be passed. The president may also veto a law passed by Congress as part of the checks and balances. Congress can get rid of the veto, but seldom does.

346/7.3

Adapted from: Hereford, J. (1998). *Passing the North Carolina Seventh Grade EOG in Reading: The Competitive Edge* (pp. 36-67). Raleigh, NC: Contemporary Publishing Company. Used by permission.

Name _____   Date   _____

Passage #17 Comprehension Questions

Structure of Government

1) Who were the Framers?

2) What are the three branches of government?

3) List two roles of Congress.

4) What is meant by "checks and balances"?

5) Who is the main person in the executive branch?

Name _____   Date _____

Passage #18: Hidden Computers

Computers were people until 60 years ago. Look up the definition in a 1940 dictionary. It will say that a computer is someone who uses numbers and data. People "computed" numbers. Computers today spend most of their time "thinking" about words. They really could be called "thinkers." They probably should be called "organizers."

Walk into any office. You will find computers sitting on all of the desks. These are called desktop computers. Desktop computers have a keyboard, monitor, and mouse. They have a printer, speakers, and cables. They are easy to see.

There are also hidden computers that hide inside another device. They are called dedicated computers. For example, a computer hides inside your digital watch. In a watch, it is "telling time." Computers hide inside your pocket calculator.

Computers hide in your Nintendo video game machine. They fix popcorn in your microwave oven. They keep your car running, and hide in your car's dashboard. A dedicated computer has only one job.

The "thinker" or dedicated computer in the microwave can be programmed to fix a meal. Somehow it knows exactly to what degree of doneness to cook. It also knows what time to stop. Just touch a few pads. While you are fixing the rest of the meal, supper is cooking. It soon will be ready to serve. Most home appliances have their own fancy microprocessor. The microprocessor in the microwave controls the timing and cooking level.

238/7.9

Adapted from: Walter, R. (2000). *The Secret Guide to Computers*. Secretfun.com. Used by permission.

Name _____   Date _____

Passage #18 Comprehension Questions

Hidden Computers

1) What was the definition of "computer" in 1940?

2) What is a "desktop" computer?

3) What is a "dedicated" computer?

4) Name three places where you could find a dedicated computer.

5) Where would you find a microprocessor in the home?

Name _____   Date _____

Passage #19: A Brief History of MP3 Players

Many years ago, the only ways to listen to music were either live, on the radio, or on a phonograph or record player. Then, owning eight-track and cassette tape players became possible and affordable. Ask a parent or teacher about those some time! Later, in the 1980s, compact discs were introduced and became popular for listening to music. As you might have noticed, each advance made listening to music easier. However, these days, there's a device that is easier than any of the others, the MP3 player!

Early on, MP3 players were a bit different than they are today. All you had to do was download songs from your computer and hit "play." One just played songs in the order that they were downloaded from the Internet, or perhaps randomly. Also, these first MP3 players held a hundred songs or less, which is more than compact discs, but still significantly less compared to now. In addition, these MP3 players did not connect very quickly to the Internet or hold movies.

Since the "early" MP3 players, several companies have developed more powerful MP3 players. These days, MP3 players can hold millions of songs and lots of full-length movies as well! Some people watch television shows on newer MP3 players. The amount of memory on a typical MP3 player is equivalent to the memory of some early super computers of about fifty years ago. MP3 players are now much faster than the first ones, too. This helps when you want to quickly scroll through and click on the song or program that you want to launch.

Do MP3 players seem too good to be true? Well, keep this in mind. You're not going to be able to purchase an MP3 player for just a few dollars. Early MP3 players, which now seem so obsolete, or out of date, used to cost nearly a hundred dollars. Now, the most basic MP3 players cost in that range; some cost more than a few hundred dollars! You'd better save your money or put in your Christmas request early.

As convenient as MP3 players are for listening to music and watching movies, that is not all MP3 players are able to do. As noted earlier, people can watch television on MP3 players. Also, teachers are beginning to use MP3 players as a part of instruction. They can record their classes and put them on the Internet for students to download. In addition, the technology used in MP3 players has been adapted for use with telephones and to receive wireless Internet service. Most cellular telephones now include MP3 players, so a person can talk and/or listen to music on them. What will they think of next?

449/8.0

Name _____   Date   _____

Passage #19 Comprehension Questions

A Brief History of MP3 Players

1) When MP3 players were first made, what were they primarily used for?

2) What features came with the first types of MP3 players?

3) Besides music, what else can newer MP3 players hold?

4) About how much do some of the fanciest new MP3 players cost?

5) How are some teachers using MP3 players?

Name _____   Date   _____

Passage #20: Are You Ready for Some Football?

Hundreds of pairs of eyes stare down at you, your teammates, and your opponents on the field. Several thousand bulbs of light shine on the field, casting giant shadows that look like massive warriors. The cameras are rolling, recording every moment of action. Your team is trailing by a touchdown, and you need one score to win. All eyes are on you and the two opposing teams. You are playing Friday night high school football.

Eleven young gladiators line up against eleven others. The objective for the offensive unit is to move the ball downfield to the end zone. The defense is attempting to vanquish the offense. All eleven people have to be on the same page for the team to succeed. For the moment, pretend that ten out of eleven players understand that the quarterback called play "A." That one person who does not know the play call could do the wrong thing, and the offense will not be able to advance. All the individuals have to work as one.

If a football team performs really well, many people praise and applaud the quarterback. The quarterback directs the offense, sometimes calls plays, throws or hands off the ball, and sometimes runs the ball. On the other hand, guess who is blamed if the offense is not successful, meaning it does not score often or enough? It's usually the individual who failed to lead the offense well. It's the same person who called the "wrong" plays, and the person who made "bad throws." In other words, it's the quarterback whom everyone holds most accountable.

Have you ever wondered why football players look so big? They wear protective pads beneath their uniforms. Why do they wear such enormous pads? Consider the following parts of football. Football players push, shove, and collide with each other, and there is a tackle on almost every play. Players are slammed on their head, yanked by their legs, and pulled down by their shoulders. Despite the protective equipment, injuries still occur during games.

As much as people watch high school football on Friday nights, the stage is even larger for the professionals in the National Football League (NFL). Millions of people watch football on television every week during the season. Stadiums for the games hold fifty to a hundred thousand people. Each year, about one hundred million people watch the championship game, the Super Bowl. In addition, the NFL is so popular that fans spend hundreds of dollars to buy their favorite players' jerseys and other related souvenirs such as hats, banners, shirts, and key chains. Perhaps the boys playing on Friday nights will be on the grand stage on Sundays in the future!

446/8.0

Name _____   Date   _____

Passage #20 Comprehension Questions

Are You Ready for Some Football?

1) What is a main reason why a football team can fail?

2) Which position on the football team often receives the most praise and the most criticism?

3) Why do football players wear pads?

4) What is the most watched football game?

5) About how many people watch the Super Bowl each year?

Name _____   Date _____

Passage #21: Skateboarding

What do you need to ride a skateboard? All you need is the skateboard itself and someone to ride it. Regardless of whether you are an early or late adolescent, or a young adult who rides skateboards professionally, it's all the same. You don't need wind or sails, and you don't need gasoline or an electrical charger either. With a solid and tenacious push, you are off and on your way.

What can you do with a skateboard? If your friend lives down the road, you could ride quickly to his or her house. In college, many students skateboard to lots of places, including from the dormitory to the classroom buildings. There are even a few professors who ride skateboards to the classes that they teach! The possibilities and destinations are literally limitless.

Have you ever seen anybody on a skateboard who had a scowl or a frown? Have you seen a crying skateboarder? I imagine you have not seen many of those! Skateboarders can do cool tricks, and they can do jumps that make other people say, "WOW!" Some people post videos of their adventures, as well as mishaps with skateboards, on the Internet.

In the 1990s, skateboarding started to become more than just a "kid thing." People like Tony Hawk and other famous skateboarders started competitions where they could skate with the best skateboarders in the world. One sports channel started showing the "X Games," which featured skateboarding. Judges rated the skateboarders' tricks and gave out prizes to those who could do the best and most difficult tricks. Millions of people watched on television, and now the "X Games" show has been on television for many years!

In a car, people have to put on seatbelts to keep from getting hurt. Now, think about what can happen on a skateboard. A person could ride over rock, catch an edge, fall, and bust his or her head. Imagine how much damage a fall like that could do! Also, skateboarders often fall on their elbows and kneecaps, causing burns. Skateboarders cannot wear seatbelts, but they are supposed to wear pads and a helmet as safety equipment.

356/8.2

Name _____   Date   _____

Passage #21 Comprehension Questions

Skateboarding

1) What are some things you *don't* need in order to skateboard?

2) How can skateboards help people in college?

3) How do most people feel when skateboarding (or watching skateboarding)?

4) In what sports event is skateboarding featured?

5) Can people get hurt riding skateboards? Explain why or why not.

Name _____   Date   _____

Passage #22: Soccer

Every four years, teams from many nations compete for the world championship of the world's most popular sport. Most of the best players throughout the world are involved in this extravaganza. Fans of the teams will pack gigantic stadiums and enthusiastically cheer on their favorite athletes. What event do you suppose this is? Is it the World Series, Super Bowl, NBA Championship, or Stanley Cup? No, it is the World Cup, soccer's premier, or most important and highest rated event.

Hundreds of millions people from around the world watch soccer. Many people are obsessed with it in European countries like England, France, and Italy, as well as in other countries, including Brazil and Zimbabwe. While soccer is becoming more popular in the United States, it is still somewhat unpopular compared to other sports. As far as viewers go, the Super Bowl, World Series, and all other major professional and collegiate championships have higher ratings than soccer in the United States.

In the past 30 years, though, these trends have changed. Many immigrants who love to play soccer have come to the United States. In addition, television has broadened the ability of people to watch soccer. Kids who have become bored with the traditional sports have discovered soccer, and more high schools offer soccer. Then, the Olympics and World Cups in the 1990s featured star players from the United States making great plays and showings. This brought in even more viewers, and even more kids wanted to play soccer, so they could be like Mia Hamm and others.

Any mention of "soccer" can bring widely varying opinions from many people. Soccer lovers talk about the tension, the tradition, and the passion that they have had since they were children. There is the excitement of the back and forth exchange, like a human chess match. Some people, though, say that soccer is boring; there's just a lot of running around and not a lot of scoring. In the United States, there seem to be more people who feel soccer is boring. In many places across the globe, however, there is nothing that competes with what is often called "futbol."

Soccer is undeniably a sport for the very fit. A full-size soccer field is longer than an American football field, and players run back and forth at nearly the pace of basketball players. The heart gets pumping, and soccer players run back and forth to get in the best position to try to score or to keep the other team from scoring. There are not as many timeouts in soccer as there are in baseball or other sports, so the athletes must endure and be in great shape. Though people are torn between whether soccer is interesting to watch, it is certainly a great sport to play to keep in shape.

468/9.0

Name _____   Date   _____

Passage #22 Comprehension Questions

Soccer

1) Which event is the most popular sporting championship in the world?

2) What are the names of two countries where soccer is very, very popular?

3) What are two reasons why more people in the United States are getting into soccer?

4) What are two reasons why soccer fans love soccer?

5) What is one benefit of playing soccer?

Name _____   Date _____

Passage #23: Movie Celebrities

Who can be known by millions but truly known by no one? Who could talk for an entire or even legendary career yet be shy in the privacy of his or her home? Does that make any sense to you? Who could seem happy for twelve or more hours a day but actually be desperately depressed on the inside? Do you give up yet? The answer is movie celebrities.

Movie celebrities may make huge sums of money but only for a price. Actors may work twelve or more hours a day when making blockbuster movies. After that, movie stars and producers have to diligently try to make their new show or movie attractive and marketable to hordes of cinema fans. On top of that, some celebrities may never truly get a vacation; fans, photographers, and journalists always approach or antagonize celebrities for pictures, autographs, or interviews. The media and fans seem to be everywhere and involved in something.

Being a movie celebrity may require many grueling hours of work, yet consider this: movie stars can make five to ten million dollars for just one movie! Not too bad, huh? Then, they can make another new movie that could make millions of additional dollars. If a star is involved in a succession of movies that all do well, that celebrity can demand lucrative contracts for every movie he or she is involved in. That all adds up to an avalanche of cash in a hurry.

Sometimes, movie celebrities are very young. They have lots of money to blow, and lots of very extravagant and expensive things that they can buy. Sometimes, people try to be friends with movie celebrities just for the money. Sometimes, these supposed "friends" can introduce destructive things like drugs to celebrities. Since movie celebrities typically are rich, they can afford harmful things like drugs. They might buy a lot of such substances. Later, the celebrities might party, do drugs, then drive or somehow get out of control, and a whole lot of trouble can come along. These things happen all too often, unfortunately, to young celebrities.

Sadly, young celebrities sometimes do not know how to handle stardom and die due to the trouble they get in. However, if celebrities can "outlive" their youth and learn from it, they can find happiness and a greater purpose for their lives. Older movie celebrities are often esteemed, or respected, by others in Hollywood and the world. Using that, older celebrities may become involved in positive causes to improve the world. They might rally people to give to others in need in this country or in another country. They might even run for political office.

444/9.1

Name _____   Date _____

Passage #23 Comprehension Questions

Movie Celebrities

1) How many hours do actors often work per day when making a movie?

2) What are two "jobs" that actors have besides making movies?

3) How much can actors make per movie?

4) What bad activities do some young celebrities get involved in?

5) What is a positive thing that some older celebrities do in their spare time?

Name _____   Date _____

Passage #24: Instant Messaging

Have you or someone you know ever been "IM'ed"? In other words, have you or someone you know ever been "instant messaged"? Probably. Millions of people across the world "IM" each other every day. For one thing, "instant messaging" works exactly as it sounds. It's a message sent to somebody instantly. If a person works on the computer, it can be mighty hard to talk on the phone and type at the same time. If a person is on an "IM" program, however, that person can work and "talk" at the same time.

The first instant messaging programs required computer users to have a unique number, similar to a phone number, which signified their identity. This required people to remember the "number" of their friends. Then, programs allowed people to make up screen names that allowed users to make up fake names that the friends could remember easier than a number. Now, most instant messaging is done on cellular phones, allowing "IM" to occur anywhere without a computer. Of course, we now call this "text messaging," or just "texting," for short.

If you have been texting a friend and need to eat dinner, you might type in "g2g, ttyl." Alternatively, if you were texting your boyfriend or girlfriend, you might type "ly☺" or "ly2☺." In other words, if you need to eat dinner, you have "got to go" or "g2g." The "ttyl" means "talk to you later." In the other example, you might tell your boyfriend or girlfriend "love you" or "love you too," or "ly☺" or "ly2☺." If you need to take a break, you could type the message "brb," or "be right back." These are just a few of the abbreviations often used in text messaging.

The instant messaging programs themselves have also become far more sophisticated. Features have been added to the programs. At first, people just typed messages and kept a list of their friends' numbers. Then, people categorized their friends in special lists. Later, new messaging programs added extra features, like animated smiling faces and beeps that let people know that someone left a message. Nowadays, messaging programs allow people to "hide" their identities so that they can seem invisible, in case they do not want someone to return a message to them.

Instant messaging is not just child's play. For example, colleges use instant messaging to allow students to communicate with librarians. Businesses use "IM" to send out mass messages about important security information. For instance, pretend that a big business was filled with people who worked at computers all day. If someone knew of a security issue, that person could "IM" or text the whole office, and everybody would know that something was happening. Also, police departments have gotten involved with instant messaging. They encourage people to register their phone numbers with the police, so that the police can send a mass instant message from the police station computer to all the cell phones registered, in case of an emergency.

497/9.3

Name _____   Date _____

Passage # 24 Comprehension Questions

Instant Messaging

1) What does "IM" stand for?

2) What is one way that modern "instant messaging" has changed from the older programs?

3) What does the abbreviation "g2g" stand for?

4) What are two new features that modern instant messaging programs have?

5) What are two ways that instant messaging can help people other than just chatting?

Notes: